—MONSTERS DO MATH!—

VAMPIRES DIVIDE!

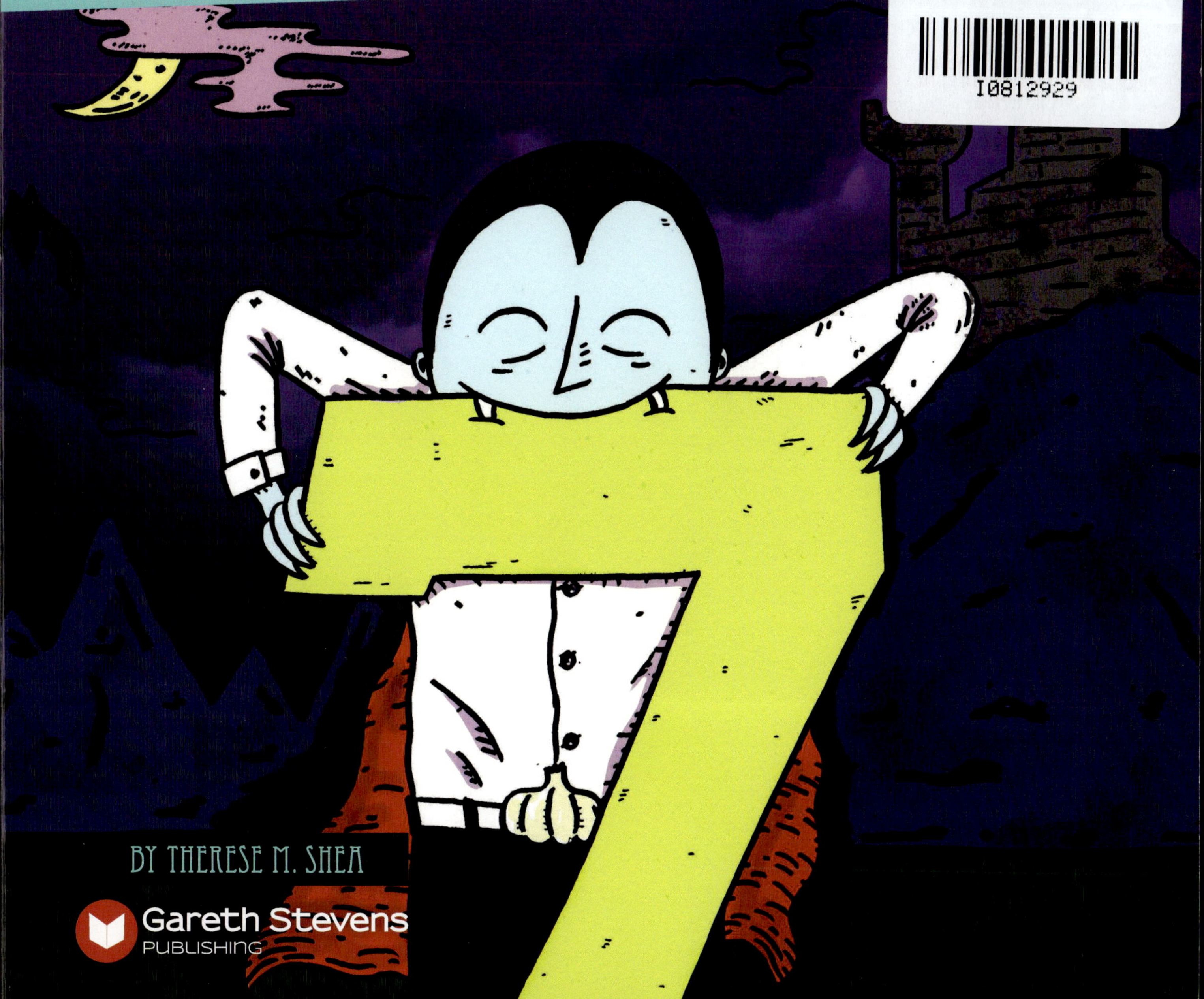

BY THERESE M. SHEA

Gareth Stevens PUBLISHING

Please visit our website, www.garethstevens.com. For a free color catalog of all our high-quality books, call toll free 1-800-542-2595 or fax 1-877-542-2596.

Library of Congress Cataloging-in-Publication Data

Names: Shea, Therese, author.
Title: Vampires divide! / Therese M. Shea.
Description: New York : Gareth Stevens Publishing, [2019] | Series: Monsters do math! | Includes index.
Identifiers: LCCN 2018014325| ISBN 9781538229354 (library bound) | ISBN 9781538233009 (pbk.) | ISBN 9781538233016 (6 pack)
Subjects: LCSH: Division--Juvenile literature. | Vampires--Juvenile literature.
Classification: LCC QA115 .S5328 2019 | DDC 513.2/14--dc23
LC record available at https://lccn.loc.gov/2018014325

First Edition

Published in 2019 by
Gareth Stevens Publishing
111 East 14th Street, Suite 349
New York, NY 10003

Designer: Sarah Liddell
Editor: Kate Light
Illustrator: Bobby Griffiths

Photo credits: p. 4 Jarp2/Shutterstock.com; p. 5 Ysbrand Cosijn/Shutterstock.com; p. 6 Hohum/Wikimedia Commons; p. 9 Pixachi/Shutterstock.com; p. 11 Mikhail_Kayl/Shutterstock.com; p. 12 Kiselev Andrey Valerevich/Shutterstock.com; p. 15 (main) Armbrust/Wikimedia Commons; p. 15 (book) Szumyk/Wikimedia Commons; p. 17 Hulton Archive/Stringer/Hulton Archive/Getty Images; p. 19 Yevhenii Orlov/Shutterstock.com; p. 20 Art65395/Shutterstock.com; p. 21 belizar/Shutterstock.com.

Printed in the United States of America

CPSIA compliance information: Batch #CW19GS: For further information contact Gareth Stevens, New York, New York at 1-800-542-2595.

CONTENTS

A Valuable Vampire 4

Name That Number 6

Divide and Conquer!......... 8

Undead Arrays 12

Toothy Tips from Vampires ...16

Leftover Garlic 18

Defeating Division...and Vampires!.............20

Glossary.................22

Answer Key 22

For More Information 23

Index 24

Words in the glossary appear in **bold** type the first time they are used in the text.

A VALUABLE VAMPIRE

A **coffin** slowly opens, and a man climbs out. He steps toward you and grins, showing two pointed **fangs**. He's a vampire!

Don't worry—he's not interested in drinking your blood. He's just waking up to help you understand a kind of math called division. In this book, he and his vampire friends will show you what division means and how to solve, or answer, division problems. Check your answers on page 22. Are you ready to sink your teeth into division?

VAMPIRES ARE FOUND IN **FOLKLORE** AROUND THE WORLD. MOST VAMPIRES ARE SAID TO DRINK THE BLOOD OF PEOPLE!

NAME THAT NUMBER

Vampires, or vampyres, are called different names in different countries. They're called strigoi (stree-GOY) in Transylvania, a famous place in Europe in vampire tales!

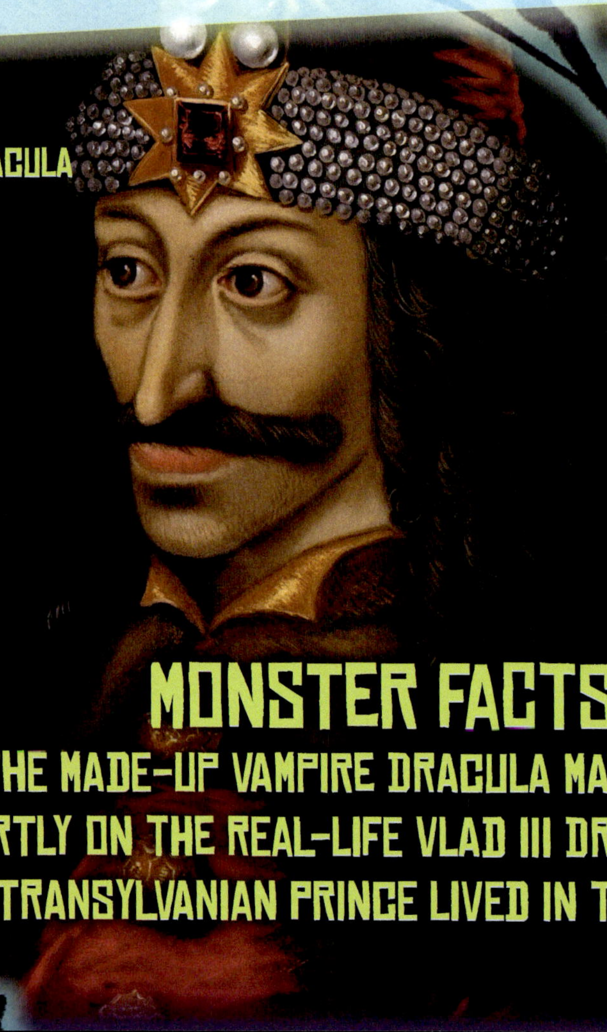

VLAD III DRACULA

MONSTER FACTS!

THE MADE-UP VAMPIRE DRACULA MAY BE BASED PARTLY ON THE REAL-LIFE VLAD III DRACULA! THIS TRANSYLVANIAN PRINCE LIVED IN THE 1400S.

Vampires have other names, and numbers in division **equations** have other names, too.

DIVIDE AND CONQUER!

It's helpful to think of division as separating a number of objects—or vampires!—into equal groups. Imagine there are 2 vampire hunters. They plan to go to a castle where 8 vampires are hiding. If each vampire hunter captures an equal number of vampires, how many will each capture?

The division equation for this problem would look like this:

8 vampires ÷ 2 vampire hunters = ? vampires captured by each hunter

or

$8 \div 2 = ?$

The picture on page 8 will help you solve this. Don't forget to check your answer on page 22!

MONSTER FACTS!

BRAN CASTLE IN ROMANIA IS OFTEN CALLED "DRACULA'S CASTLE."

Vampires can help you when you're faced with any division problem, if you think of it like a story. Let's see how:

$$15 \div 5 = ?$$

Here's a story: There are 15 vampires. They divide into groups of 5 to play a game. How many groups are there in all?

Make up a story for this division problem and solve it:

$$42 \div 7 = ?$$

MONSTER FACTS!

THERE'S AN EASY WAY TO TELL A VAMPIRE FROM A HUMAN. A VAMPIRE WON'T APPEAR IN A **MIRROR**!

UNDEAD ARRAYS

Most tales say that vampires are dead people that have come alive again. These "undead" rise at night from their coffins. You can use coffins to understand division.

An array is a grouping of objects—or coffins!—in rows of equal size.

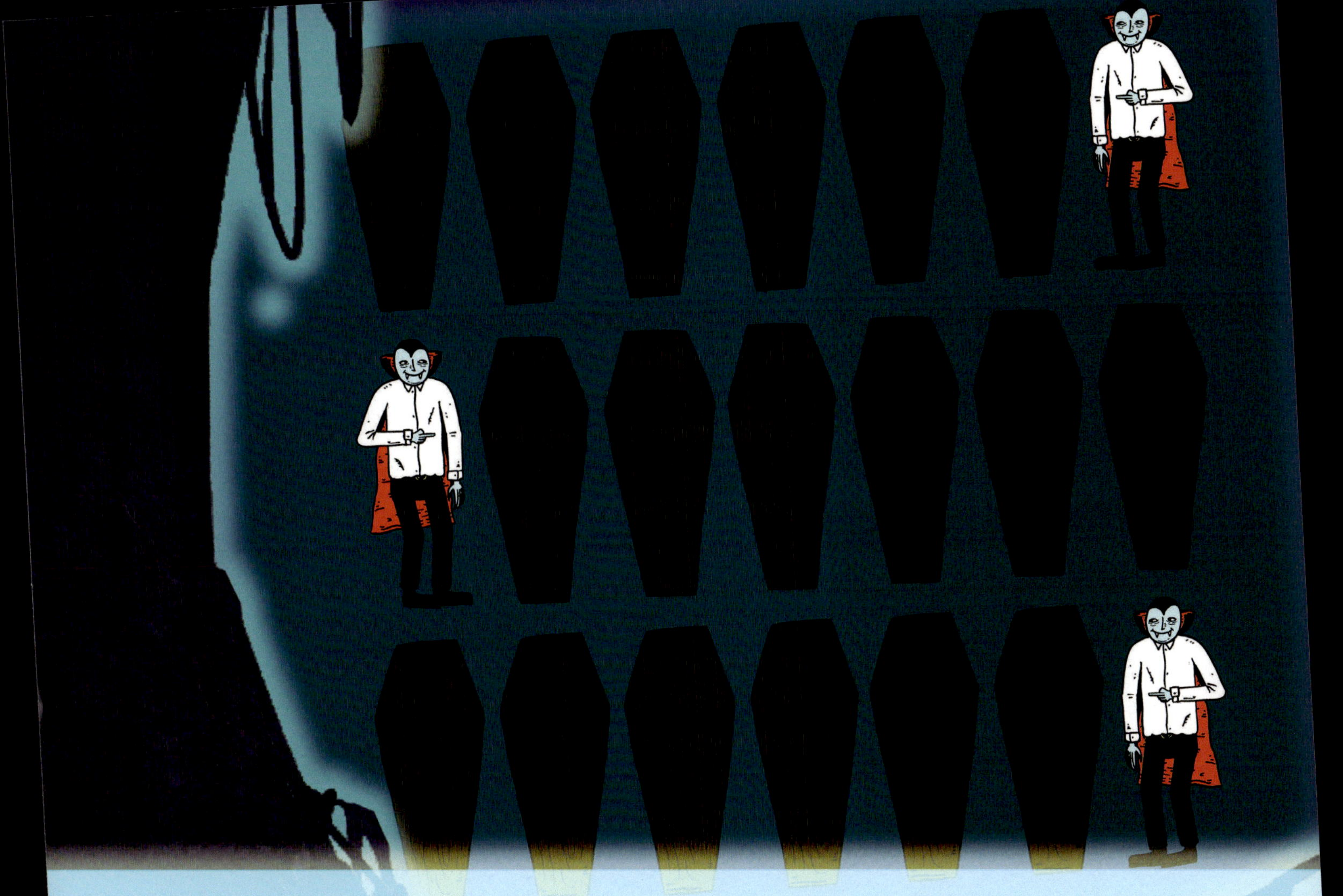

Eighteen coffins are divided equally among 3 vampires. How many coffins does each vampire have?

18 coffins ÷ 3 vampires = ? coffins each

You can find the answer to the division problem by counting the number of coffins in any row of this array.

There's a party at Dracula's castle, and 25 vampires are going. They arrive in 5 groups. Each group has the same number of vampires. How many vampires are in each group?

Create your own array to solve this problem:

$$25 \div 5 = ?$$

1. On a piece of paper, draw a number of equal-sized boxes that matches the divisor: 5.
2. In each box, draw a tiny picture.
3. Keep adding one picture at a time to each box until you've completed the number of pictures equal to the dividend: 25.
4. The number of pictures in each box is the quotient, your answer!

MONSTER FACTS!

THE MOST FAMOUS VAMPIRE STORY IS BRAM STOKER'S *DRACULA*. IT WAS PUBLISHED IN 1897. MOST VAMPIRE STORIES AFTER THAT ARE BASED ON PARTS OF THIS BOOK!

TOOTHY TIPS FROM VAMPIRES

There are some easy tips for some division problems.

Anytime you divide a number by itself, the answer is 1.

$$18 \div 18 = 1$$

Anytime you divide by 1, the answer is the same as the dividend.

$$21 \div 1 = 21$$

MONSTER FACTS!

VAMPIRES ARE SAID TO WAKE UP AT NIGHT TO HUNT FOR BLOOD. THEY MUST RETURN TO THEIR COFFIN OR GRAVE BEFORE THE SUN RISES—OR THEY'LL BURN UP!

Use both tips to answer these two problems:

$9 \div 1 = ?$

$14 \div 14 = ?$

LEFTOVER GARLIC

Sometimes, numbers can't be divided evenly. Whatever's left is called the remainder. Let's see what remainders mean in the world of vampires!

Vampire hunters know **garlic** keeps vampires away. Three vampire hunters have 13 **bulbs** of garlic. They try to divide the bulbs among them equally. How many will each have?

You know 13 cannot be divided exactly into 3 groups. Each vampire hunter gets 4 garlic bulbs. One bulb is left over.

$$13 \div 3 = 4 \text{ with a remainder of } 1$$

Imagine 4 vampire hunters divide 26 garlic bulbs among themselves as evenly as they can. How many will each get? How many will be left over? Draw an array if you need to.

MONSTER FACTS!

MANY TALES SAY THAT ONE WAY TO KILL A VAMPIRE IS TO DRIVE A WOODEN STAKE THROUGH ITS HEART!

DEFEATING DIVISION... AND VAMPIRES!

Vampires exist in real life! But they're not people—they're animals. Perhaps the most famous is the common vampire bat. It mostly feeds on the blood of livestock.

Division problems exist in real life, too. Whether you're trying to divide a pizza among your friends or figure out how many buses your school needs to take a field trip, division can help. There's much more to learn about vampires and division. Now you have tools and knowledge to apply to the problems you face next!

SOME FOLKLORE SAYS THAT VAMPIRES CAN TURN INTO BATS!

GLOSSARY

bulb: a rounded part of some plants that is under the ground

coffin: a box in which a dead person is buried

equation: in math, a statement that two things are equal

fang: a long, pointed tooth

folklore: ideas or stories that are not true but that many people have heard or read

garlic: a plant related to the onion that has small sections (called cloves) which have a strong taste and smell

mirror: a piece of glass that shows the image in front of it

ANSWER KEY

page 9: 4 vampires captured by each hunter
page 10: 3 groups
page 11: 6
page 13: 6 coffins each
page 15: 5 vampires
page 17: 9; 1
page 19: 6 with a remainder of 2

FOR MORE INFORMATION

BOOKS

Kenan, Tessa. *It's a Vampire Bat!* Minneapolis, MN: Lerner Publications, 2017.

Mahaney, Ian F. *Math on Halloween: The Properties of Multiplication and Division*. New York, NY: PowerKids Press, 2013.

Wingard-Nelson, Rebecca. *Ready for Division*. Berkeley Heights, NJ: Enslow Publishers, 2014.

WEBSITES

Division and Remainders
www.mathsisfun.com/numbers/division-remainder.html
Read more about division and remainders.

Division
www.brainpop.com/math/numbersandoperations/division/
Watch a movie about division.

Publisher's note to educators and parents: Our editors have carefully reviewed these websites to ensure that they are suitable for students. Many websites change frequently, however, and we cannot guarantee that a site's future contents will continue to meet our high standards of quality and educational value. Be advised that students should be closely supervised whenever they access the internet.

INDEX

array 12, 13, 15, 19

bats 20, 21

blood 4, 5, 17, 20

castles 8, 9, 14

coffins 4, 12, 13, 17

dividends 7, 15, 16

divisors 7, 15

Dracula 6, 9, 14

Dracula 15

equations 7, 9

fangs 4

folklore 5, 21

garlic 18, 19

mirrors 11

quotients 7, 15

remainders 18, 19

Transylvania 6

vampire hunters 8, 9, 18, 19

wooden stakes 19